LETTING GO

A Holistic
and Meditative Approach
to Living and Dying

by
RICHARD W. BOERSTLER
Practitioner in Thanatology

ASSOCIATES IN THANATOLOGY
206 Maplewood Street
Watertown, Massachusetts 02172

Associates in Thanatology is part of a charitable tax-exempt collective of health professionals, educators and psychotherapists who are exploring new and innovative ways of assisting dying people. Lectures and workshops are available.

ISBN 0-9607928-0-5-T

LIBRARY OF CONGRESS CATALOG CARD NO. 81-71653

REVISED EDITION 1982
COVER PHOTO BY AUTHOR.
PERMISSION TO REPRINT IS GRANTED. PLEASE CREDIT SOURCE.

ASSOCIATES IN THANATOLOGY
206 MAPLEWOOD STREET
WATERTOWN, MASSACHUSETTS 02172
(617) 923-9278 • (617) 259-8936

THE WAY THINGS ARE

The Way has neither Beginning nor End. But in the course of this eternal and circular flow, individual things die and are born. The perfection of these ever-flowing things cannot be relied upon (and is not an absolute perfection). Being empty now, full at the next moment, nothing remains in one state even for a moment.

The years cannot be kept back; time cannot be stopped. Now decaying, then alive; now replete, then empty; ending is immediately followed by a beginning. Such is the interminable flow of all things. The life of existence in this world of things is like a horse galloping and rushing along. With every movement they change; at every moment they shift.

What could you at all do (against this universal change of things)? Whatever you may do everything will go on naturally transforming itself.

—*Adapted from Chuang Tzu, Inner Chapters XVII*

Chuang Tzu, who existed in about the middle of the fourth century B.C., was the central thinker of Taoist thought of ancient China. The writings attributed to him are summed up in a single word: freedom. This freedom will be evident in the approaches to life and death in this book.

CONTENTS

ILLUSTRATIONS

PREFACE

This book grew out of a series of talks and demonstrations given over the past three years at universities, hospitals, churches, and hospice groups. Some of the material has also been taken from videotapes of television interviews.

Most of the text arises out of my confrontation with death in the course of my work as a practitioner in thanatology. This confrontation has taken place both at the bed-side of the people I have served and within my own psyche as I searched for the realities of life at death.

The excerpts quoted in the text are from some of my teachers past and present. I recently founded the Associates in Thanatology, a study and therapy collective in the Boston area.

My first teacher, Suzuki Roshi, once said, "The truth is always near at hand." I will try to describe what has been "near at hand" for me during these confrontations with death.

Instructions in these psycho-spiritual methods is provided for the sick and their families without charge. We invite your support of this much needed work. No religion, no philosophy, no medical model will dominate our search for new and innovative ways to assist dying people. We call attention to the question of Robert M. Veatch who asks, "Is death moral?" He continues,

> People are no longer able to return to the simple solutions of the past. They are no longer able to participate in a simple religious healing ceremony supported by their communities or to let nature do its own healing without their domination. Cannon's "Wisdom of the Body" has been superseded by the wisdom of technology. . . . We have lost almost entirely the art of self-medication, ceding these operations to the medical priests. Now countless hopelessly ill and suffering patients literally cannot avoid death-prolonging intervention.[1]

INTRODUCTION

This book presents holistic methods for the transformation of consciousness during living and dying. The methods described are authentic ancient practices which are revolutionary in terms of Western ideology and philosophy. Our concern will be to harmonize life and death. The practices are non-sectarian and involve no dogma or belief system.

In my practice in thanatology I have been joined by Hulen S. Kornfeld, R.N., who as a former head nurse in a chronic disease hospital has been present at "the passage" on many occasions. Thus in this introduction I have used the plural "we" to describe our joint endeavors.

Modern science tells us in the theory of particle physics that the entire universe is in a continuous state of flow or flux. All life and matter are part of a continuous cosmic transformation. Our present life is only a fleeting moment in the great flow of reality. In this knowledge lies our liberation from the anxieties and fears of life and death which will lead to our continued growth and spiritual evolution.

This book will focus on the nature of this reality and set forth concepts and practices which will allow us to understand and experience these transformations. In particular, it will call attention to the equation between our inner self and our outer world. We will see that these two are functions of each other, and that each observer is an integral part of the continuous process of eternal change.

In order to be able to consciously experience this transformation, we offer a method of working with the conscious mind never before published. The practice comes to us via the oral tradition from Tibetan medicine. We call this psycho-spiritual procedure "co-meditation."

Some years ago in the course of my spiritual search I studied with the Clear Light Society of Boston where I learned of this co-meditation method during my internship with this group. Ms. Patricia Shelton, the founder of the society and I appeared together on Hubert Jessup's, "New Heaven/New Earth" program, A.B.C.-

T.V., Boston, on March 12, 1978 and the first television demonstration of the "co-meditation" method was given by Ms. Kornfeld and myself on the same program on January 25, 1981.

I had broken away from the oral transmission practices of the Clear Light group by publishing the first edition of "Letting Go" in 1979. Ms. Shelton told me she had received this authentic practice from a Tibetan Lama, and was most unhappy that I had broken the chain of oral transmission.

The deep serenity and peace that I observed using this procedure with terminally ill patients and others in acute anxiety has made me realize that the observed results cannot easily be explained by Western medicine and psychology. We recently began a pilot study of the method at New England Medical Center in Boston and are continuing to encourage all research and study of this ancient transpersonal technique (please see epilogue).

The word "meditation," now used so often in the West, is not an adequate translation of the time-honored practice of a breathing discipline long known in ancient Yogic and certain mystical traditions. "Meditation," in current usage, implies thinking about something (e.g. meditate on a problem), whereas the meditative procedures of the East lead to a cessation of thought.

Co-meditation will be presented as a powerful and tested method for bringing about "peaceful heart and clear mind" even with individuals who have *never* meditated before. The procedure is a transpersonal one, meaning it must be taught by, and done with, a friend or guide on a one-to-one basis. The method provides a deep calming of the conscious mind and body, which is not addressed by Western psychology. In the West psychotherapy tries to change the *contents* of consciousness, while meditation transforms consciousness itself. The practices as set forth in this book are part of a most practical approach to both living and dying in terms of a holistic understanding of the universe.

Physiologically, the process is a sharing of the subject's rhythm of respiration by a guide, to reduce and finally dissolve the subject's anxiety and stress more profoundly than any therapy.

The book is organized into three sections: (1) a holistic view of the universe, with illustrations of the cosmos accompanied by some musings; (2) a description of meditation and its relationship to body-mind transformations occurring at the time of death; and (3) complete instruction in the procedure of co-meditation, and discussion of its use in modern thanatology.

As practitioners in thanatology, we are vitally interested in improving and enhancing every aspect of patient care during the "last days." For three years we have offered co-meditation to patients requesting assistance with the acute anxiety associated with terminal illness.

We became interested in altered states of consciousness during the dying process as we became aware that a fundamental need of dying patients was not being met: that of transcendence and identity, which has often been put aside during the course of a lifetime. Brother David Steindl-Rast (*Parabola,* Vol. II, #1, 1977) describes it as the need to find meaning at the time of death, when life no longer seems to have purpose. He points out that even when we come close to death and all purpose slips out of our hands, our life and death can still be meaningful.

Our work with the dying indicates that a most powerful way of centering and helping the patient find meaning, especially in acute anxiety conditions, is through the use of the breath in a deeply shared pattern of respiration. The practice we use has evolved around the use of breathing in a psycho-biological manner. The technique brings to the patient the known psychological and physiological effects of the meditative state even in people who have never meditated before. These effects include deep body and muscle relaxation, alert mental state, lowered metabolic rate, slower heart and respiration rate, lower oxygen requirement, lower lactate blood levels, increase in GSR (galvanic skin response), and increase in alpha brain wave. These effects have been reported by patients and caregivers to whom we have taught co-meditation. The deaths that have occurred in this state have been reported by caregivers as peaceful, serene, and even ecstatic. For the caregiver, co-meditation provides an essential task, sharing in the process of dying with the patient. The helpless feelings which generate remorse and guilt are prevented.

It is difficult, in our youth-oriented, death-denying culture, to deal with old age, sickness and death. Statistics show that four out of five people in the United States die in hospitals and nursing homes. Most of us will die in an institution rather than at home; many of us will endure the process of dying without meaningful support. Western medicine and psychology do not provide much support for the dying.

However, there are ways of dying with dignity, just as there are ways of living with dignity, and we will explore them. In addition, we will discuss the relationship of meditation to the dying process as well as providing instruction in co-meditation, which provides a state of profound relaxation.

It is said that death is the moment of supreme spiritual opportunity. Through these transpersonal practices we will explore the possibility of transforming consciousness in the pre-mortem state. First, however, we will look at a holistic view of the universe.

I.

A HOLISTIC VIEW
OF THE UNIVERSE

*When the sage of Concord, Henry David Thoreau, was said
to be sick, one of the townspeople came to visit him and
asked him if he had made his peace with God. Thoreau
answered, "I never knew I had a quarrel with him."*

Amaury de Reincourt, in his book "The Eye of Shiva," states:
"The new universe disclosed by Einstein's relativity presents itself
as a continuous whole made up of interrelated *events,* prompting
A. N. Whitehead to state that the event is the unit of things real."
These events are determined by the geometric properties of the
"field" where they occur. Classical physics had conceived of an
empty space extending indefinitely in all directions and an equally
empty time without beginning or end, but totally separate from
space: both were presumed to be pre-existent to matter, both
logically and by implication, chronologically. No more. The universe of classical physics has been swept away by relativity, the
main hallmark of which is *unification,* joining together in an
indissoluble continuum space, energy and matter."[2]

1

This unification of the universe may be conveyed visually. Some illustrations follow, along with some musings to accompany each. These set forth the oneness so often described in the writings of religious mystics and now by modern physicists.

The first image is of the cosmic web which describes Nature in terms of energies and their interactions. We ask that the reader focus on each picture for a few moments before reading the musings that follow. In Section II we offer a definition of death which will be enhanced by the reader's understanding of the ideas suggested by the pictures. Take the time to become familiar with them.

The Cosmic Web (Figure 1). The universe is described as a seamless web of unbroken movements and changes, filled with undulating waves and patterns of ripples and temporary "standing waves" like a river. Every observer is an integral function of this web. It never stops; it never turns back on itself. No event or process ever repeats itself exactly and none of its patterns are real in the sense of being permanent, even for the briefest moment of time. This immense web of rolling change does not itself change. It is called the uncarved block, devoid of any definable shape. The mother, matrix of time, including being and non-being, the present, the future, the vanished past, the great whole of continuous duration, infinite space, infinite change.[3]

Kuan Yin (Figure 2). "Kuan Yin is the ancient Chinese symbol of the World Mother, and it is representative of the feminine principle of creation; the Mother aspect of Deity. The feminine principle has been repeated throughout history by many names— Mother Kundalini, Shakti, Mother of the Universe, World Mother, Virgin Mary, Isis, Ishtar, Sophia, etc. To the Gnostic Christians She was known as the Holy Spirit, one of the Divine Triad; but ecclesiastical Christianity has regarded the Holy Trinity as entirely masculine, thus depriving its adherents of a sublime and ennobling concept."

"The unfolding 'New Age', foretold by prophets (and referred to by religions), has as its keynote the conscious restoration of the

Fig. 1. The Cosmic Web

Golden Balance between the feminine and the masculine principles. This 'Golden Balance' is to be found in the hearts of all people, and though called by many names, it is none other than the True 'Self'. As people throughout the world enter into cooperation with these Divine Principles, the 'New Age' will be made manifest."

Know this 'Balance' by honoring its source, which is the True 'Self'.

> Love is your very nature . . .
> GOD DWELLS WITHIN YOU AS YOU. At times we are the formless way (the mother). Then we are also the myriad transformations of the world (the child). Know the mother that you may know the child. Know the child that you may return and hold fast to the mother. Then as long as life lasts nothing can harm you.[4]

Yin-Yang (Figure 3). The identity of and indivisibility of spirit and matter, according to ancient Chinese philosophy, is the basic structure and pattern of the universe. In the second century B.C. Huai Nan Tzu said, "He who conforms to the course of the way (Tao), following the natural processes of heaven and earth, finds it easy to manage the whole world."[5]

Cyclic change and flow is in this view of the world the essential nature to be observed by man. When all actions are thus to be directed by this constant polar reversal and circular flow man becomes "one with the way," living in complete harmony with nature, and succeeds in everything he undertakes.

This ancient diagram of the symmetric arrangement of the dark yin and bright yang is not static but in continuous movement, with the yin in fullness then giving way to the yang returning to its beginning. Here the meditating Buddha is contrasted with the equations of modern physics. Thus we are suggesting that the theorems and models of the physicist are in perfect harmony with the views of Eastern mysticism. It is said that those who have experienced this harmony begin to understand the ancient Chinese saying: "From the creative yang and receptive yin emerge the 10,000 things"—dark/light, night/day, cold/hot, soft/hard, wet/dry, winter/summer, shadow/sun, female/male, etc.[6]

Fig. 2. Kuan-yin

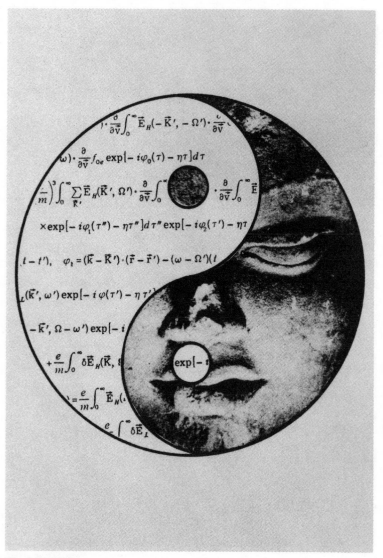

Fig. 3. Yin-Yang

Fig. 4. Dancing Shiva

Shiva's Dance (Figure 4). The descriptions of the universe in modern particle physics are now becoming so close to some ancient Hindu views of the world that we offer here the most popular Indian god, Shiva, king of the dancers. In this cosmology all life is part of a "great rhythmic process of creation and destruction of death and rebirth, and Shiva's dance symbolizes this eternal life-death rhythm which goes on in endless cycles.

"At the same time, Shiva reminds us that the manifold forms in the world are illusory. His gestures wild and full of grace, precipitate the cosmic illusion; his flying arms and legs and the swaying of his torso produce—indeed, they are—the continuous creation and destruction of the universe, death exactly balancing birth, annihilation the end of every coming forth."[7]

"In the night of Brahman, nature is inert, and cannot dance until Shiva wills it: he rises from his rapture and dancing sends through inert matter pulsating waves of awakening sound, and lo! matter also dances, appearing as glory round about him. Dancing he sustains its manifold phenomena. In the fullness of time, still dancing he destroys all forms and names by fire and gives new rest. This is poetry but nonetheless science."[8]

A second and more dramatic musing is the following poem.

Shiva: The Power of Transformation

Shiva!
Thou storming destroyer of the world!
Thou transforming transformer!

Thou, who giveth and taketh within one breath
Release me from myself!
Dissolve the form into freedom:
Undo this life earth-rooted
Undo this life of craving
Undo this life of clinging!

Deliver me from the death of stagnation
To the storm of life:

The storm that uproots all craving
The storm that defies all clinging
The storm that breaks down what resists!

Deliver me from a life that negates death,
O thou eternal transformer
Thou dancing liberator of the universe.[9]

Life and Death

What is a good death?

What is the fundamental need of the dying person?

If your own mind is destined to become the universe itself at the time of death, what state of consciousness do you wish to be in at the moment of passage?

We begin our seminar on meditation and the dying process with these three questions.

Death (not dying) is said to be the one thing that man has not corrupted. In a holistic view, the passage appears to be happening in the same way it has since prehistoric times.

In the context of our society, the first question suggests that the pre-mortem conditions in which many people have found themselves in have certainly been less than desirable. The fundamental need at the time of death must vary from one person to another. In the West, we often list external or outward conditions we believe might be desirable or relatively pleasant, such as dying in a hospital, on a mountaintop, by the ocean or alone in the forest. Unfortunately, in Western culture we have looked outward for so long that we are uncomfortable with most introspective approaches. The United States was founded by explorers who were always looking outward. Later we conquered the West and built a huge industrial empire, and still going outward we began a costly exploration of outer space. It was only some fifteen years ago that the drug culture started to describe a new territory, that of inner space. Many of us are uneasy in these areas of altered states of consciousness, even those such as meditation and yoga.

We will find that meditation addresses the question of transformation of consciousness at the time of death. We will describe and teach (in Part III) practical methods for changing your own consciousness, to be used by the healthy as well as by the dying. These methods will give you a state of profound relaxation, a peaceful heart, and a clear mind, which will help you answer the important question—"Who am I?"

This question must be answered by you sometime before your death. Western medicine will not help you answer it, nor will psychology, except by explaining you as a bundle of conditioned responses. The sociologist would talk about your identity in terms of tribal development. The biologist would describe your physical structure. Yet it is the *essence* of *you* and *"you-ness"* that is your *consciousness;* and it is this *"you-ness"* you must try to reach and be fully aware of.

Before examining the ancient meditation practices that will help you reach your "you-ness" we will take an overview of our psycho-spiritual state, using the ideas and musings set forth at the beginning of this section.

Harmonizing Our Life and Death

This approach is not, as many Westerners suppose, to be resigned to fate, but rather to restore physically within the self man's primordial condition. Once this return to the origin is achieved, a simplicity in oneness occurs, and the fear of death is removed.

The most beautiful affirmation of death (perhaps in all literature) can be found in the writings of Chuang Tzu (399-295 BC). He believed that life and death are human distinctions made by those who do not understand the unity of all things. He said: "The ten thousand things are one with me. Nothing is not acceptable, not even death. The sage leans on the sun and moon, tucks the universe under his arm, merges himself with things and achieves simplicity in oneness. For him, the ten thousand things are what they are, and thus they enfold each other. Life is the companion of death, death is the beginning of life. Who understands their workings? Man's life is a coming together of breath. If it comes together, there is life; if it scatters, there is death. If life and death are companions to each other, then what is there to be anxious about?

"The great clod (the earth)," continues Chuang Tzu, "burdens me with form, labors me with life, eases me in old age, and rests me in death. So if I do think well of my life, for the same reason I must think well of my death.

"You have the audacity to take on human form, and you are delighted, but the human form has ten thousand changes that never come to an end. Your joys then must be unaccountable. Therefore, the sage wanders in the realm where things cannot get away from him and are all preserved. He delights in early death; he delights in old age; he delights in the beginning; he delights in the end."

When Chuang Tzu was about to die, his disciples wished to give him a sumptuous burial, but Chuang Tzu said, "I will have heaven and earth for my coffin and coffin shell, the sun and moon for my pair of jade discs, the stars and constellations for my pearls and beads, and the ten thousand things for my parting gifts."

After his wife had died, Chuang Tzu was reproached for beating on a bowl and singing. But he replied:

"When she had just died, even I could not remain unaffected. But then I reflected that in the beginning she had been without life. In fact, she had not only lacked life, she had no form. Indeed, she had not only lacked form but also lacked breath. In the mingling of the waste and chaos, with one change there came breath, with another form, and with yet another life. Now with still another change she goes in death. This is like the movement of the four seasons, from spring to autumn, from winter to summer. Now, when she lies sleeping in the great dwelling if I were to start bawling and bewailing her, I would merely show that I did not understand destiny."[10]

Is Death A Lie?

I suggest death is a lie which cannot exist except in the context of another lie, the ego. Because we believe we *are,* death appears to exist. Our understanding of death resides not in death itself but in the death of the ego. In the unconscious mind the ego disappears, and simultaneously death disappears. The real you is eternal and is not born nor does it die.

One way of looking at life is by studying the ocean. Realize that we are individually waves in the ocean, and if we look deep into the waves we see the ocean which always is, and of which we are always a part. Conceptually we have invented death in deciding to identify with the ego. Like the waves of the ocean, there never was, nor will there ever be, a separate ego, except in our minds. Thus I say we invent death since it is impossible in the nature of things. We are just changing forms. Where is the child you once were? Did the child die? Only the form has changed. In old age have you died? Age has brought widsom and its own beauty. The old man dies and the body disappears but consciousness continues. And God did not happen, God is happening and will continue to happen. Do we not create God every day? In this new dimension of God we are not just seekers but also creators. This is particularly true in terms of our consciousness. This is the significance of the *Tibetan Book of the Dead,* which is really a manual for the living! It is concerned with both the intermediate states between birth and death and those between death and rebirth. In the Middle Ages there were many texts with titles like "The Craft to Know Well to Die," subtitled, "Know well how to die for you shall not learn to live unless you learn to die." Perhaps we can now see that what we call death is not a direct experience, but a concept—a concept deduced by observation of an external event. In reality there are two things that cannot be experienced: our ego and our death! If death were real we could experience it, but as long as we are experiencing anything we are not dead!

To help us see this matter of not experiencing death, here is an account of a Japanese religious scholar who suffered many years with a terminal illness. He left a very unusual manuscript, "Death in Life." Being driven to find answers, he hopelessly tried to intellec-tualize about life hereafter. He tried in vain to accept his fate, using the religious knowledge he had accumulated. Then one day he had a flash of illumination. He wrote: "The one thing necessary is our preparation to confront death when it comes. What I discovered was that I was afraid of death because I was thinking I would experience it. And then I discovered that death was outside my experience. What we can experience is only life and living. It was a shocking experience for me to realize that there is no other way permitted for humans to live except to keep living." His account concludes: "Death is simply the lack of life."[11]

A Definition of Death

At the beginning of this section we offered four portraits of the universe whose theme was that all matter and life are in a continuous state of flux and flow. Now we are ready to fit a definition of death into this theme.

The essence of this theme is that we and the universe are in a vital process or rhythm and we must begin to become fully aware of this process by identifying ourselves consciously with it.

We will thus be able to experience the very nature of life and death by surrendering to this rhythm instead of interfering with it. The key to identifying with the life flow about and within us is the breathing process, which we will explore in the next section.

In order to fit our life and death into this holistic and synergistic system, we will use the definition of death given by the German-born Lama Anagarika Govinda. In his chapter on "Impermanence and Immortality," he writes:

> Life means giving and taking; exchange; transformation. It is breathing in and breathing out. It is not taking possession of anything, but a taking part in everything that comes in touch with us. It is neither a state of possession nor of being possessed. Neither a clinging to the objects of our experience nor a state of indifference but the middleway, the way of transformation.
>
> We are transformed by what we accept. We transform what we have accepted by assimilating it. We are transformed by the act of giving, and we contribute to the transformation of others by what we are giving.

13

He who opposes this process will die the slow death of rigidity; he will be expelled and rejected from all that lives, like dead matter from a living organism. *Death is a deficiency of the faculty of transformation.*

In the acceptance of this definition of Death, we must see that we are really talking about life! To live, we must go through continual change, which might be called a continual death. Thus, we are really courting death when we refuse to accept it. We enjoy a waterfall or cloud formation—in spite of its impermanence: the changing forms heighten our delight.[12]

A most beautiful description of a waterfall is given by Suzuki Roshi:

I went to Yosemite National Park, and I saw some huge water-falls. The highest one there is 1,430 feet high, and from it the water comes down like a curtain thrown from the top of the mountain. It does not seem to come down swiftly, as you might expect; it seems to come down very slowly because of the distance. And the water does not come down as one stream, but is separated into many tiny streams. From a distance it looks like a curtain. And I thought it must be a very difficult experience for each drop of water to come down from the top of such a high mountain. It takes time, you know, a long time, for the water finally to reach the bottom of the waterfall. And it seems to me that our human life may be like this. We have many difficult experiences in our life. But at the same time, I thought, the water was not originally separated, but was one whole river. Only when it is separated into many drops can it begin to have or to express some feeling. When we see one whole river we do not feel the living activity of the water, but when we dip a part of the water into a dipper, we experience some feeling of the water, and we also feel the value of the person who uses the water. Feeling ourselves and the water in this way, we cannot use it in just a material way. It is a living thing.

Before we were born we had no feeling; we were one with the universe. This is called "mind-only," or "essence of mind," or "big mind." After we are separated by birth from this oneness, as the water falling from the waterfall is separated by the wind and rocks, then we have feeling. You have difficulty because you have feeling. You attach to the feeling you have without knowing just how this kind of feeling is created. When you do not realize that you are one with the river, or one with the universe, you have fear. Whether it is separated into drops or not, water is water. Our life and death are the same thing. When we realize this fact we have no fear of death anymore, and we have no actual difficulty in our life.

When the water returns to its original oneness with the river, it no longer has any individual feeling to it; it resumes its own nature, and finds composure. How very glad the water must be to come back to the original river! If this is so, what feeling will we have when we die? I think we are like the water in the dipper. We will have composure then, perfect composure. It may be too perfect for us, just now, because we are so much attached to our feeling, to our individual existence. For us, just now, we have some fear of death, but after we resume our true original nature, there is Nirvana. That is why we say, "To attain Nirvana is to pass away." "To pass away" is not a very adequate expression. Perhaps "to pass on," or "to go on," or "to join" would be better. Will you try to find some better expression for death? When you find it, you will have quite a new interpretation of your life. It will be like my experience when I saw the water in the big waterfall. Imagine! It was 1,430 feet high![13]

With the above definition of death we are ready to look at the life-death transformations going on about us and their relationship to the breathing process, meditation and death.

II.

MEDITATION AND DEATH

Consciousness is deathless since it belongs to a plane of
reality that is beyond life and death as well as beyond time
and space—death being merely the withdrawal of con-
sciousness from the space-time universe of phenomena that
we can observe from the outside. What dies and is reborn,
however, is the expression of consciousness
that is organic life.
—The Eye of Shiva, *Amaury de Riencourt*

We in the West have been flooded with gurus, meditation masters, swamis, teachers, yogis, etc., and it is no wonder we are perplexed about the word "meditation." Some of us believe that "contemplation of one's navel" is not for us, not knowing that the yogi sitting in full lotus position is often taking only one breath per minute. So what? we may comment. But what most Westerners also may not realize is that the yogi is not concerned with his physical state or contortion ability, but is vitally aware of his mental state or consciousness. In psychiatric jargon, his mind is clear and his

17

ideational response is reduced to little or no thought activity. In mystical terminology, his consciousness has merged with the universe and his thoughts, if any, are few and sporadic.

As we mentioned earlier, the word meditation, now used so glibly in our culture, is not an adequate translation for the authentic and disciplined breathing practices long described in Yogic meditative traditions. Meditation to most means to concentrate or focus on something, whereas the meditative practices in most Eastern traditions require transcending all conceptual thinking. Generally meditation is a mini-death to the mind and deeper than physical death. Meditation is like consciousness without the mind—an open sky with no walls surrounding it—and is a subtle death of the "I," "me," "mine," of your ego and all that defines you. All that remains is pure consciousness.

The mental processes of thinking are not meditation, and so-called intellection is actually an obstacle to meditation which has been called a dropping of the walls of the mind. We could say that during meditation, mind with a small m dies and mind with a capital M goes on living.

Generally all religious mystical traditions, such as the Christian Trappists, Judaism's Hasidics, Islam's Sufis and the Buddhists' Zennists, have had long experience with meditative and altered states at the time of death. Some ancient cults have employed drugs, breathing exercises, mantras and prayers all with the intent of transforming consciousness at this moment of great opportunity. For example, the Christian would be transported into the Kingdom of Heaven and the Buddhist into Nirvana. Perhaps the next step in evolution is the most acceptable explanation for most people.

In the West we do not seem too concerned with the "spinning mind" of anxiety and fear long addressed by the above traditions. But patients in a large modern hospital know only too well when someone in the next bed or in their unit has died, and at night their minds often race or spin with fear and anxiety.

I often see golfers and tennis players practicing their strokes for hours at a time, and I wonder about our most precious gift of consciousness and how bankrupt many of us have become in our mind practice. It has been said that the untrained mind is like a wild monkey jumping from tree to tree, or a one-armed rider on a wild blind horse!

The hypothesis upon which our approach rests is as follows: A certain state of mind will evoke a particular mode of respiration, and conversely, a certain mode of respiration will evoke a particular state of mind.

All traditional meditation practices are concerned with breathing procedures. Examples include the chanting of prayers, the use of rosaries, and mantra and other yogic disciplines.

Psychotherapy has recently become interested in meditative disciplines. Psychotherapy's primary focus has been changing the contents of consciousness, whereas meditative traditions have been concerned with the transformation of consciousness itself. Psychotherapy has left behind its origins in the psyche and focused on rats, mazes and behavior. The separation of psychology from religion may prove to be one of the most dangerous dichotomies of our civilization, since it creates the illusion that we have progressed beyond the spiritual wisdom of earlier times.

In the next section we will try to heal that dichotomy with instructions for working with consciousness in the pre-mortem state. To understand this procedure, we need to look at the physiology of breathing and its relationship to consciousness.

Physiology and Meditation

Much research has gone on since 1972, when *Scientific American* first published an account of Benson's and Wallace's finding about correlates of physiology and meditation.[14] Zen masters, yogis and practitioners of transcendental meditation (TM) were monitored for metabolism, heart rate, brain wave, oxygen consumption, and blood pressure. Tests indicated that meditation produced effects in the body through the control of an "involuntary" mechanism, the autonomic nervous system. Since then many investigators have confirmed these findings. In 1977 another study of meditation was reported in *American Scientist*. Herbert Benson and others found that meditative states produced marked effects on the autonomic nervous system.[15] Western medicine has long sought a way to influence the sympathetic and parasympathetic actions of the autonomic nervous system; the studies cited above seem to provide scientific proof that meditation is one such way. This has profound importance to the validation of the benefits of altered mind and body states.

We suggest that in the holistic view of the world the three major components of the universe are mind, consciousness and breath. Let us look at these components and their relationship:

1. Breath appears to be the pulse of the mind and thus there is a direct correlation between breathing and thinking.

2. Breath connects all life with consciousness. It is said that in meditation and mantra chanting there is a crossing of the sea of the mind. From a psychological point of view, this is the bridge from the conscious to the unconscious mind. (This is most important in working with patients in coma.)

3. It has been noted in ancient traditions that we are born on an inhalation and we die on an exhalation. In one cosmology it is said that life is measured not by the number of years but by the number of breaths. Theoretically we could count our daily breaths and project our life expectancy.

4. When we experience sudden fear and shock, we feel it in the solar plexus. No intellectual or central nervous system is needed here. Our breath or lack of breath tells us all.

Earlier we referred to the dropping of the walls of the mind during meditation. With this occurs what disciplined meditators have called the "great death," meaning the death of the ego. We experience the essential self as being nothing. We know the self is not graspable, and for perhaps the first time in our life see into this no-thingness, and find that it is empty and void. The place thought and felt to be occupied by "me" is quite full of space. Instead of the imagined "me" it is clearly seen that there is no-thing. This complete reversal of the view of oneself as the experiencer is reflected in the reversal of everything experienced. Although the world is just as it was before, it is now seen differently. Everything is (as it were) turned upside down and inside out. I am not so much in the world as the world is in me.

Following the "great death," meditators may go through what has been called the "great nakedness," which is simply being one with what is, or becoming completely at one with the present moment.

I think we can see how important this state of mind may be in late terminal illness, when the consciousness of the patient needs to be clear and centered, not scattered and anxious. When a deep meditative state does prevail, a synthesis occurs which allows the patient to experience the whole body and mind. Thus breathing (meditation) becomes a practical method of having a spiritual experience, the breath being the mediator between body and mind. This may become the first step in the final transformation of consciousness. The "letting go" process must proceed naturally at this time. We must return to our native state of the pure and shining voidness, without objects, specific consciousness or identity, without past, present or future.

When death comes naturally, it is part of a gradual process of disintegration. A summary of this process would include the dissolution of the psychophysical constituents of form, feeling, thought, volition and consciousness. The heart would cease beating and a fainting might occur. At this point a clear light has been reported by many of those who came close to dying, but were saved.

In the dying process, meditation is of supreme importance in helping us realize that all flows, all changes, all transforms (see Section I). The Buddha once said, "Everything is impermanent, like autumn clouds. The birth and death of beings is like the scenes of a drama. Human life is like the flash of lightning in the sky or like the waters of a mountain stream."

Perhaps it is now apparent why we place such emphasis on the third question in Section I: If your own mind is destined to become the universe itself at the time of death, what state of consciousness do you wish to be in at the moment of passage?

Below is a most moving and beautiful account of the transformation and passage from Aldous Huxley's monumental treatise on living and dying, *Island*.

Rounding a screen, he caught a glimpse . . . of a high bed, of a dark emaciated face on the pillow, of arms that were no more than parchment-covered bones, of claw-like hands. . . . He looked at the face on the pillow . . . still, still with a serenity that might almost have been the frozen calm of death. . . .

"Lakshmi," she said again more loudly. The death-calm face remained impassive. "You mustn't go to sleep."

. . . "Lakshmi!"

The face came to life.

"I wasn't really asleep," the old woman whispered. "It's just my being so weak. I seem to float away."

"But you've got to be here," said Susila. "You've got to know you're here. All the time." She slipped an additional pillow under the sick woman's shoulders and reached for a bottle of smelling salts that stood on the bed table. . . . Then after another pause, "Oh, how wonderful," she whispered at last, "how wonderful!" Suddenly she winced and bit her lip.

Susila took the old woman's hand in both of hers. "Is the pain bad?" she asked.

"It would be bad," Lakshmi explained, "if it were really my pain. But somehow it isn't. The pain's here; but I'm somewhere else. It's like what you discover with the *moksha*-medicine. Nothing really belongs to you. Not even your pain."

. . . "And now," Susila was saying, "think of that view from the Shiva temple. Think of those lights and shadows on the sea, those blue spaces between the clouds. Think of them, and then let go of your thinking. Let go of it, so that the not-Thought can come through. Things into Emptiness, Emptiness into Suchness. Suchness into things again, into your own mind. Remember what it says in the Sutra. 'Your own consciousness shining, void, inseparable from the great Body of Radiance, is subject neither to birth or death, but is the same as the immutable Light, Buddha Amitabha.'"

"The same as the light," Lakshmi repeated. "And yet it's all dark again."

"It's dark because you're trying too hard," said Susila. "Dark because you want it to be light. Remember what you used to tell me when I was a little girl. 'Lightly, child, lightly. You've got to learn to do everything lightly. Think lightly, act lightly, feel lightly. Yes, feel lightly, even though you're feeling deeply' . . . Lightly, lightly—it was the best advice ever given me. Well, now I'm going to say the same thing to you, Lakshmi . . . Lightly, my darling, lightly. Even when it comes to dying. Nothing ponderous, or portentous, or emphatic. No rhetoric, no tremolos, no self-conscious persona putting on its celebrated imitation of Christ or Goethe or Little Nell. And, of course, no theology, no metaphysics. Just the fact of dying and the fact of the Clear Light. So throw away all your baggage and go forward. There are quicksands all about you, sucking at your feet, trying to suck you down into fear and self-pity and despair. That's why you must walk so lightly. Lightly, my darling . . . Completely unencumbered."

. . . He looked again at the fleshless face on the pillow and saw that it was smiling.

"The Light," came the hoarse whisper, "the Clear Light. It's here—along with the pain, in spite of the pain."

"And where are *you?*" Susila asked.

"Over there, in the corner." Lakshmi tried to point, but the raised hand faltered and fell back, inert, on the coverlet. "I can see myself there. And she can see my body on the bed."

"Can she see the Light?"

"No. The Light's here, where my body is." . . .

"She's drifted away again," said Susila. "Try to bring her back."

Dr. Robert slipped an arm under the emaciated body and lifted it into a sitting posture. The head drooped sideways onto his shoulder.

"My little love," he kept whispering. "My little love . . ."

Her eyelids fluttered open for a moment. "Brighter," came the barely audible whisper, "brighter." And a smile of happiness intense almost to the point of elation transfigured her face.

In the fleshless face the mouth had fallen cavernously open, and suddenly the breathing became stertorous.

"My love, my little love . . ." Dr. Robert held her more closely. "Let go now, let go. Leave it here, your old worn-out body, and go on. Go on, my darling, go on into the Light, into the peace, into the living peace of the Clear Light . . ."

Susila picked up one of the limp hands and kissed it, then turned . . .

"Time to go," she whispered . . .[16]

Letting Go

It is said that humans are most like God in one aspect, that of creativity. Our discussion of meditation and death has now brought us to look at the power of the mind during the final transformation. Let us hear Govinda again:

We complain about the impermanence of the world and of our own corporeality as long as we do not know that we ourselves have created them. But he who knows that throughout eternity we have created our innumerable bodies and the worlds experienced through them, will bemoan the transiency of these creations as little as the singer will grieve over the vanishing notes of his song since he knows he can recreate them whenever he wishes.

Herein lies the secret of immortality: we are immortal not by holding on, but by letting go. Whatever we master, we need not cling to; we can always create it anew, thanks to the creative power of the sovereign spirit within us.

Do not the flowers awaken every spring? Nature is lavish due to its creative power. Only the uncreative mind clings to the solid-ified dregs of life.

The mere belief in an immortal soul, or the conviction that something in us survives death, does not make us immortal unless we know what it is that survives and that we are capable of identifying ourselves with it. Most human beings choose death instead of immortality by identifying themselves with that which is perishable and impermanent, by clinging stubbornly to the body or the momentary elements of the present personality, which they mistake for the soul or the essential form of life.

Differently expressed: immortality is within our reach but like a poor man who does not know that a treasure is hidden in his house, we are not able to make use of it. If we do not know of what immortality consists, it is as useless as a buried treasure— and even more so if we know that it exists and do not know where to search for it.[17]

And now the secret of your own consciousness at the moment of death! Hear the words of Taoist master Tseng:

The mind of one who returns to the Source thereby becomes the Source. Your own mind is destined to become the universe itself! You see your body as a flower born to bloom, to give forth fragrance, to wither and to die.Who would care for a peony that stayed as it was for a lifetime, for a thousand or ten thousand years? A mere cabbage would be worthier of attention. It is well that things die when worn out, and no loss at all, for *life* is immortal and never grows with the birth of things or diminishes with their death. A worn-out object is discarded, life having ample materials to supply the loss. Now do you see? *You* cannot die, because you have never lived. Life cannot die, because it has no beginning or end. Becoming an immortal just means ceasing to identify yourself with shadows and recognising that the only "you" is everlasting life.[18]

We have been concerned in this section with the meditative aspects of the dying process. Meditation was described as the most profound means of "letting go," which we all must do sooner or later. We are speaking primarily of the possessions of the mind: lust for power, money, prestige, virtue, knowledge, even spiritual experience.

It has been said that all the sacred teachings of the world could be summed up in two words: "Let go." Just let go—don't hold on to anything—not people, things, ideas, or notions. Just moment to moment, let go. And have a clear mind and a peaceful heart.

This idea is summed up beautifully in a Japanese poem by Shinso:

Does one really have to fret about death?
No matter what road I travel I'm going home.

25

An interesting comment by Alan Watts on *not* "letting go" is included here:

> Some people are always afraid if they let go, the devil will take over first, unaware that *not* having let go *is* the devil already in full control. For ordinary self-control is the domination of one's behavior by the selfish self; its love is assumed, pretensive, and dutiful; its righteousness is hypocritical; its chastity issues in cruelty; its spiritual ideas are highbrow ways of inflating the ego; its profuse confessions of sin are subtle ways of one-upping more ordinary people; and its beneficence has an odd way of arousing resentment in its recipients.[19]

In the following section, we offer profound holistic transpersonal techniques to deal with the pain and anxiety that may flood the consciousness during a life-threatening illness. The techniques may also be used by anyone, sick or healthy, who wants to center their spinning mind and achieve serenity.

III.

CO-MEDITATION AND ITS USE
IN MODERN THANATOLOGY

Let your life lightly dance on the edges of time
like dew on the tip of a leaf.
— Rabindranath Tagore

This section is an instruction manual in co-meditation for physicians, nurses, hospice volunteers, family members, and primary care givers for the terminally ill. After the guide has shared the breathing procedures with the patient several times, he or she should locate a nurse or family member, someone who has close day-by-day contact with the patient, to be brought to the bedside and taught these methods.

If you or your friend, family member or patient has a life-threatening illness, there is something you can do to help.

(Note: The following introductory comments through page 29 are specifically for the terminally ill.)

27

Starting to Let Go

You have just learned that your physical condition (or your loved one's or patient's) is very serious; medical treatments have been exhausted, and the prognosis is guarded. Medical science cannot heal the disease you have, and your condition is terminal. You may or may not know how long you have left to live.

After hearing this prognosis, you are naturally in a state of shock and panic. You ask if anything more can be done medically, and the answer is no. After long days and nights of fear and anxiety, you have to some degree accepted your situation: you understand you are going to die, you are living with this knowledge, and you are dealing with it.

First Things First

You may have already completed personal and financial business and wonder what's next. If you have a religious adviser, you may have been given much comfort and help. What now is your most fundamental need?

You may have already determined that heightening your own consciousness is a strong need, and if you wish to learn of tools to do so, you have already taken the first step. It is possible to experience death with dignity and nobility. Your death is the moment of great spiritual opportunity. Through meditation, you can reach the deepest levels of awareness within you.

> The dying process as described by the great mystics is a more complicated situation than we might think. It is not sudden: it is a gradual withdrawal of consciousness from the body into the Self. First, consciousness is withdrawn from the senses to the mind. The senses shut down, and outer awareness of the body and of our surroundings is gone. We still have ears, but we hear nothing, because consciousness has been withdrawn. We still have eyes, but there is nothing outside that we see.
>
> Yet, though we can no longer see or hear, there is still consciousness in the mind with all its desires and regrets, all its hopes and fears.

This process is strikingly parallel to what happens in meditation when we have withdrawn consciousness from the senses. The crucial difference is that in meditation, the withdrawal is voluntary, whereas in death, it is involuntary. We can in meditation go even further by deliberately withdrawing consciousness not only from the senses but also from the mind. This is what stilling the mind means. Yet as long as the mind has not been stilled through meditation, consciousness will remain in the mind at the moment of death. We will then still be identified with the ego.[20]

Ideally, if our transformation has been complete, and our ego has merged into the cosmic flux of the universe, the transition to our next state will flow quite naturally. As mentioned earlier, we should be started early on our "Letting Go" process, and should proceed into the final stages with peaceful heart and clear mind.

Most Profound Means of Letting Go

Meditation is the most profound means of "letting go," and the following instructions will describe some very powerful and ancient methods for achieving these most serene and beautiful states, hopefully before the moment of our death.

These practices may be instituted by a guide on a one-to-one basis with patients who have never meditated before. It is the transpersonal aspect that characterizes these practices as most spiritual and revolutionary. Sharing the breath of another person during this transformation of consciousness is a most sacred and profound experience. We will now see how this is accomplished.

The direct correlation between breathing and thinking has been noted for centuries by Eastern yogis, gurus and meditation masters. It is said that breath connects all life to consciousness.

> If mind and breath are functioning properly, negativity will not arise. It is important to become conscious of our breath. When breath is not balanced, many thoughts and concepts arise. If our breath is like an expansive lake with very still water, this lake reflects the things around it beautifully. If we disturb this lake by throwing a rock into it, the lake can no longer reflect the things around it beautifully: an image is no longer formed. So we can

29

discover what disturbs us by watching our breath.

The less we breathe, the more calm we become. It is this calm inner breath which we can use to transmute us into blissfulness. The more we relax into this breath, the more we will find that this breath is *energy*. There can be much meaning within this breath. It can produce tremendous positive feelings.[21]

Co-Meditational Practices

These methods may be described as co-meditational practices, introducing a shared breathing pattern between the patient and guide. After introductory relaxation suggestions, the guide concentrates on the breath of the patient, and from then on the guide has no breath of his/her own.

For the guide as well as patient, the procedures produce a rapid drop in respiration and create a profound state of relaxation. The concomitant slowing down of thought activity is naturally most important to the dying patient. Other psychological and physiological responses will undoubtedly be found. We encourage all serious investigative and research undertaking. (Please see diagram on page 31.)

Religious Dogma

There must be no imposition of *any* religious dogma, creed, or belief system on the patient's mind, body or spirit. In terms of psychotherapy, the therapist/guide will have absolutely *no goal* for the patient, especially at this crucial moment of his or her life/death situation. What guide, therapist, nurse, clergyman, or physician would assert his or her omniscience when the patient's fate is balanced so delicately between heaven and earth?

Thus, it must be clear that there is no attempt to "lay any trip" on the patient, either philosophically or therapeutically. The guide is just totally present with the patient—to share a profound experience of the universe, that of breath, the elixir of life, without which none of us would be on this planet.

Obviously, there are no judgments, beliefs or opinions involved

Diagram of Transpersonal (Co-Meditation) Practice in Thanatology

Instructions

GUIDE

A

(1) *Visual focus on chest and diaphragm of patient and—*

(2) *Verbal sounding (see text) on each exhalation of patient.*

PATIENT:

B-C

One requirement— to listen to the sound of guide's voice. (Nothing else is required)

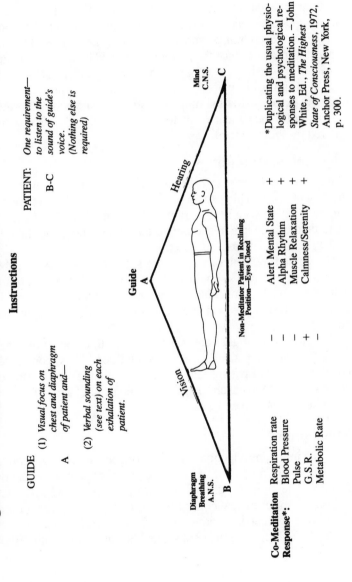

Mind
C.N.S.
C

Hearing

Guide
A

Non-Meditator Patient in Reclining
Position—Eyes Closed

Vision

Diaphragm
Breathing
A.N.S.
B

Co-Meditation Response*:		
Alert Mental State	+	
Alpha Rhythm	+	
Muscle Relaxation	+	
Calmness/Serenity	+	
Respiration rate	−	
Blood Pressure	−	
Pulse	−	
G.S.R.	+	
Metabolic Rate	−	

*Duplicating the usual physiological and psychological responses to meditation. – John White, Ed., *The Highest State of Consciousness*, 1972, Anchor Press, New York, p. 300.

in a transpersonal, breathing procedure with another human being, and it is possible that this experience may become one of the most relaxing and deep transpersonal moments of the patient's life.

Most important, once the method is learned by a family member or friend, he or she may continue the technique after the guide has left. In all probability, it will be a family member, nurse or friend who will be present at the time of death. This method will provide the matrix for the patient's transformation of consciousness, so long ignored by Western medicine.

Physical Surroundings

The room should be warm. Light should be dim, particularly over the patient's face. Thirty to forty-five minutes should be set aside for complete quiet, with no interruptions. Though it is not critical, no more than two people in addition to the patient and guide should be in the room, to minimize distractions.

The guide should sit or stand close to the bed at a position about even with the patient's shoulder. He or she should obtain a comfortable stance without touching the patient during the meditation. The guide must be in a position to observe the patient's diaphragm, chest and face.

The procedure might continue for two or three hours or longer, depending on the patient's wish and condition. Thus, comfortable positions for both patient and guide are desirable. If interruptions occur (such as medical checks) they should be brief and with as little discussion as possible.

The Guide

After the initial introductions, a period of general low-level conversation might or might not be indicated before beginning the sharing process. The guide should be in a calm, centered, and open state, and observant of the patient's physical, mental and spiritual needs. (This book will not deal with suggested training requirements for the guide; the only requirement considered is that the guide must move into the patient's life situation with complete openness to and acceptance of whatever he or she may encounter.)

The Patient's Role

It is assumed that the patient has never had any experience with meditation, yoga, or other breathing-related practices. If a patient has a religious practice of his or her own, this must be encouraged; if a spiritual advisor is present, he or she should be encouraged to remain. The methods presented here do not involve or conflict with any belief system or religion. (The guide will steer away from discussion of religion, philosophy, or after-death experience; this is not a "talking-out" approach.)

It is assumed that the patient has now heard about the practices here described and has called the guide to give help and instruction. If the patient is ambulatory, he or she may lie flat on the floor with no pillow. A bed or couch is also suitable if not too soft and if the hands can be free and resting straight beside the thighs, palms up. The eyes should be closed and remain so during the entire session.

Clothing should be loose and shoes removed. If the patient is on the floor, he or she should be kept warm with a blanket, kept smooth over the chest and stomach area, so that the respiration may be seen. If convenient, the toes should be pointed away from each other.

By this time, the patient probably no longer wants to talk, only to learn what the guide has to impart. Thus, no further conversation will take place: the only verbal communication will be the instructions of the guide, which will continue during the meditation.

Patient's Breathing Pattern

The guide will first direct his or her attention to the patient's breathing pattern. It is here that the guide's experience and training will be most useful. If the guide is experienced in observing his or her own breathing, it will be much easier to relate to the breath of the patient. If the patient's breathing is rapid and irregular, the guide will employ one type of breathing procedure; if it is slow and regular, another type will be more appropriate. We will describe these methods later on.

Relaxation

A series of relaxation suggestions may now be given. Generally, these are basic muscle relaxations, starting with "Relax the toes," continuing to the ankles . . . knees . . . hips . . . pelvic area . . . stomach . . . chest . . . shoulders, and so on to the scalp . . . forehead . . . eyes . . . mouth . . . chin, and finally, the whole body. . . .

After the patient has relaxed, a brief observation of the chest and diaphragm areas should be made. If respiration is rapid, the guide should proceed with another method of meditation designed to calm the mind and body described below.

Calming the Mind and Body

The guide will do this by addressing the patient by name and saying the following:

". . . we are now going to share an ancient method of calming the mind and body. There is nothing to fear. I am going to remain beside you for the entire visit. You will not be alone.

"Now then, while your eyes remain closed, I want you to pay close attention to the sound of my voice. There is nothing else you have to do except listen carefully to my voice and to follow your own breathing. Listen carefully to my voice—it will be close to you from now on.

We are now going to begin, together, the great sound of 'Letting Go,' the sound of 'AH' sounded out and strung out like this: 'AAAAAAAAAAAHHHHHHHHHHH.' We are going to say it together on the out-breath exhalation only."

Here the patient may be given a choice: although encouraged to join the guide in the sounding of the "AH," he may choose to rely on the guide's sounding if he prefers. The instruction then continues, with the guide saying:

"Please now think of nothing but our (my) sound(s) of 'Letting Go' and listen closely again to the sound(s) of my (our) voice(s). Thinking is not necessary; just sound the 'AH' and drop everything else from your mind."

The 'Letting Go' Sound

"Just the sound of my voice and your breathing," the guide continues. "Just the 'AH' and your own breathing, just the 'Letting Go' sound.

"After ten to twelve soundings of the 'AH' you may stop saying it and only listen to my voice as I sound for you the most powerful sound of our body, the sound of 'Letting Go,' the sound of 'AAAAAHHHHH.'"

The guide has now focused his attention on the lower chest area to observe closely—with 100% attention—the breathing (exhalation) of the patient. At the beginning (top) of the exhalation, he should pinpoint the commencement of the out-breath and begin sounding the "AAAAAHHHHH" and adjust it exactly to match the respiration rate of the patient.

To do this, the guide must assume a comfortable position near the patient and continue total concentration on the exhalation . . . sound aloud continuously the "AAAAAHHHHH" so that the patient may clearly hear the vocal union of the guide's sounding with the exhalation perception (breathing out) of his own body.

This first breathing meditation may continue for twenty to thirty minutes, with the guide's breathing pattern in total union with the patient's respiration, the guide continuing to focus on the patient's chest area so that each exhalation of the patient becomes the exhalation of the guide, the guide always following (as in a dance) the rhythm of the patient.

If the patient's breathing is too rapid and the "AH" procedure not appropriate, other methods should now be considered. Second choice will be the method called "Counting the Breath."

Counting the Breath

The relaxation instructions are the same as before, and the guide should now begin close voice instructions to the patient, again addressing the patient by name, as follows:

". . . now we will begin a series of very powerful methods for calming the mind through the breath. Listen, please, very carefully to my instructions, paying close attention to the sound of my voice. We will start to count your "out" breaths (exhalations) going from one to ten and then repeating the series.

"On each 'out' breath, I will do the counting for you, and all that is necessary for you to do is to follow with your mind and breathing the exact number we are at. With your eyes closed all the time, I want you to be relaxed and to pay close attention to my voice. That is all I want you to do.

"As we count along, you may find it helpful to visualize a large white number—one, two, three—appearing over your head with each count I give you. This may help you focus on each breath and number as I count them for you. Remember, *thinking is not necessary*, only close attention to each number. Remember, just breathing and counting . . . just counting and breathing . . . just breathing and counting . . . just counting and breathing . . . Let us now begin on each out-breath."

As with the "AH" method, the guide will then watch closely the rise and fall of the patient's chest and diaphragm. Beginning with an exhalation, the guide will sound the numbers "One" through "Ten" clearly and crisply, so that the patient's breath and the counting become one. The counting might continue for an extended period of time.

Sometimes the guide could give some "Letting Go" remarks, only on the exhalation, such as:

"Peaceful heart, clear mind."

"Breathing and counting, counting and breathing."

"Concentrate on the sound of my voice."

"See the numbers, clear and white, going out over your feet to the horizon."

But generally, the fewer extraneous thoughts and comments, the better.

If the patient should fall asleep, you will notice a change to a more rapid breathing pattern. This is perfectly all right. Simply discontinue counting and sit with the sleeping patient until he or she wakes up. Then consider using one or more of the methods again.

At this point, the patient might be started on a particular chant or mantra, depending on his or her religious preference.

Mantras for a Chronically Ill Patient

"Mantra" (or "mantram") is a Sanskrit term signifying a sacred word, verse or syllable which embodies in sound some specific deity or supernatural power or energy. The following is a method of using the mantra with the chronically ill patient.

First, mantras, like music, can help in crossing the sea of the mind, from the conscious to the unconscious, and a mantra will produce the most profound effect if used continuously. Thus, it is the guide's responsibility to introduce this ancient practice at a time when it will be most helpful and meaningful to the patient. However, the choice must always be the patient's, though the guide may offer encouragement.

The guide will act as a facilitator suggesting only that the patient look to his past or childhood for some early influence. If Christian, he may choose the Jesus Prayer of the Heart: "Lord Jesus Christ, have mercy on me." Jewish patients might use the ancient "Sh'Ma" ("Hear, oh Israel, the Lord our God, the Lord is one.") Buddhists might use "Om Mani Padme Hum."

These mantras or prayers should be chanted together, always on the out-breath if possible, over and over again while the guide is there, and perhaps later on a cassette when the patient is alone. Too, a family member, friend, or nurse can be asked to chant with the patient when the guide is not present.

The mantra may be chanted close to the ear for at least 30 minutes after "clinical death." Sound is the last sense to leave the body, and the dying process is always gradual (See page 28).

The peace of mind that the patient's very own mantra may bring is of great importance, especially late at night when the mind may speed up with worries and fears. It is important to remember that the mantra never misleads: it does not seek the solution of a problem but rather the dissolution of impediments, the loosening of knots into which we have entangled ourselves by our own desires, prejudices, and attachments.

To employ a mantra repeated either by the patient or by an attending guide is of supreme importance at the moment of death. The practical significance of this has not been understood by doctors, psychologists or theologians generally for many centuries. If our last thoughts are ego centered, there will be no way to avoid the suffering of ego identification when the body is wrenched away; but if, the great mystics say, we are able to repeat our mantra at the moment of death, we merge into the cosmos just as a bursting bubble becomes one with the sea.

Summary

I have described the optimum surroundings in hospital, hospice or home situations for experiencing an ancient and authentic cross-meditational practice to bring about peaceful heart and clear mind.

Three ancient methods of sharing the breath are set forth to be used under various conditions. The great universal sound of "Letting Go" (the Throat Chakra) on the exhalation of the "AH" sound is described in detail. "Letting Go," which is said to be the essence of all religions, is shared on a one-to-one basis in a deep transpersonal meditation by the guide, who concentrates on the rise and fall of the patient's chest area.

A second ancient cross-meditational practice, similar in purpose and technique to the first, is the counting of each exhalation in a sequence from one to ten and then repeating the series. The guide focuses on the out-breath and sounds the number to the patient, who is instructed to listen closely. The patient is also instructed to visualize a large white number against a black background each time the number is sounded by the guide. This counting method is preferable when the patient is anxious, disturbed, and fearful, and when the breathing is irregular. Both methods are indicated to bring about a profound state of relaxation and serenity.

Finally, a mantra of the patient's choosing is used to still the mind in those cases where the other two methods may not be suitable. Also, the mantra chanted by patient and guide together may be recorded on cassette tape for lonely hours at home or in the hospital. It is especially meaningful to use the patient's own prayer or mantra to calm the mind at night and when minimal response or participation is expected from the patient due to coma, drugs or other pre-mortem conditions. It is suggested that the chanting of a mantra may permit a crossing between the conscious and unconscious mind, producing a deep and profound relaxation.

The mantra may also be chanted at the time of death and even if the patient is asleep or in a coma. This chanting gives the family and close friends something meaningful to do while spending this special time with the patient.

The following verses may be helpful in integrating the methods described above:

> The Kingdom of Heaven is Within You.
> *. . . Jesus*

> With a Quiet Mind,
> Come into that Empty House,
> Your Heart, and Feel the Joy
> Of the Way beyond the World.
> *. . . The Dhammapada*

> Search for the Inner Light,
> And do not give up
> Until this goal is achieved.
> When you have reached that Light,
> You cross the Boundaries of Death.

> Death means the Transformation of
> Our physical conditioning and
> Not the extinction of Ourselves,
> The Transformation of our Life
> Into its Elemental Conditions.
> *. . . Mystery of Death*

CONCLUSION

Following Govinda, we defined what is erroneously called death as "a deficiency in the faculty of transformation." If we can accept this definition and fit it into a holistic framework of the cosmos, we will have come a long way from the Western notion that death is like an evil spirit, or the wicked witch, who must be driven from the community.

We might learn to look at life as does the Sioux medicine man, Lame Deer, who told us that the Sioux sometimes look at a beautiful spring day when the sun is out and say, "You know, today would be a great day to die!" The reason for this idea is that they wanted to integrate the death experience even at the point of greatest enjoyment of the physical beauty of the world, and the things which will be left behind at the point of death—"yes, I can even die here!"

Thus, an understanding of this is like a lifelong preparation for death, which is, in fact, a deepening of the experience of living itself.

EPILOGUE

We include here a brief description of some beautiful beings who have transformed into their next state using these methods.

Usually we have been called by a family member, nurse or aide who has heard of our approach to anxiety and fear. In most cases we have been consulted in late terminal conditions, where the spinning mind seemed to escalate beyond all rational limits.

We have introduced this co-meditative approach with chronic and terminally ill patients as part of a transpersonal procedure of sharing the patient's breathing pattern. We initiated the procedure with selected patients as time permitted, suggesting a thirty-minute treatment period and, if possible, repeated daily. When practical, the nursing staff, hospital aides, and family were instructed in this method.

After the introductory period, an assessment was made, using the rate of respiration as a guide to the degree of relaxation. The subject of death was discussed with patients only at their request. Patients with *no* meditative experience were selected as follows: (1) those who were cooperative and willing to participate; (2) those who were responsive and alert; and (3) those who were able to remain in a supported position for about thirty minutes in a quiet setting between medical checks and feeding.

One memorable mother and son provided us with many deep insights into the dying process. Death is always the great teacher. A 31-year-old male with metastasized cancer of the spine was being cared for by his mother with the help of home nursing aides. He was a poet and very clear mentally but had many unresolved philosophical issues as he approached death. We were introduced to him about ten days before his transformation and found him reaching out to us for nurturing of any sort. We explained some of the approaches set forth in this text and shared the method with his mother, who had hypertension, and then with him. He was responsive to it and asked his mother to work with him between our visits. We also taught him a mantra using a visualization of light as well. He was particularly fond of the latter.

When early one morning his death was near, he asked his mother

41

to repeat his mantra for him and for some time she shared it on his exhalation, until he stopped breathing. His transition was peaceful, serene and without anxiety, but the beauty of this event with the mother giving the chant to her son at this moment cannot be overstated. She thus became an intimate part of his evolution both at his birth and at his death. The fact she *could do something* was most important to her and all those in the household.

We submit that the method of co-meditation should be examined in light of its holistic implications for the whole family unit. The method involves the personal, psychological investment of another human being, perhaps for an extended period of time. In a high technology society such as ours this may require a deep transpersonal sharing not available in the usual hospital or clinical setting. In this connection the hospice movement must continue to evolve into the fabric of our culture.

Another being we were privileged to assist was a 59-year-old man with inoperable lung cancer, confined to a hospital. His anxiety was severe, as was his wife's. His breathing became even more difficult and his respiration rate went up to 48–50 per minute. We instituted the procedure with alternate guides taking turns following the breath using the counting method. His respiration dropped to normal within a few minutes. He drifted into a coma and died peacefully a few hours later. His wife was most appreciative of the changes we effected with him.

Recently we also shared this procedure with a beautiful young couple. The husband had lung cancer and was severely agitated with a rapid breathing pattern. His anxiety was so marked that we could only employ a mantra or chant of "love," which his wife continued to verbalize on his exhalation. She chanted this mantra with him during his last hours and told us that he died in a very peaceful state. As always, we do not impose our word or mantra, but ask the patient to find a short, meaningful phrase from the past, such as a poem, psalm or prayer. If this can be repeated by successive family members, it will be of inestimable value during the last hours or days.

These practices have been known since the Middle Ages, especially in the Eastern rite of the Christian church. The "Jesus prayer" has been practiced and chanted for centuries, with the mind-stilling properties reported on in depth in church literature and elsewhere. For a complete description and history of this, see "St. Gregory Palamas and Orthodox Spirituality" by John Meyendorff.[22]

I am currently engaged in encouraging all aspects of research in the use of co-meditation. Studies in autonomic nervous system response and in the physiology of pain are showing that stress reduction is a necessary modality in modern health care.

A lecture and demonstration is available for hospitals, universities, nursing schools, hospices and medical support groups. The Associates in Thanatology (206 Maplewood Street, Watertown, Massachusetts 02172, (617) 623-9278, (617) 259-8936) is also available for consultation for patient care in grief, loss, pain and death education. If you would like more information about this work, please contact the author.

NOTES

1. Veatch, Robert M., *Death, Dying and the Biological Revolution,* Yale University Press, New Haven, 1976.

2. Reincourt, A. de, *The Eye of Shiva,* William Morrow & Co., New York, 1981.

3. Rawson, P. and Legeza, L., *Tao,* Bounty Books, New York, 1978.

4. Quan Yin, S.Y.D.O., P.O. Box 994, Ojai Valley, California 93023.

5. Quoted in Needham, J., *Science and Civilization in China,* Vol. II, p. 51, Cambridge University Press, Cambridge, England, 1956.

6. Capra, F., *The Tao of Physics,* Shambhala, Berkeley, California, 1975.

7. Zimmer, H., *Myths and Symbols in Indian Art and Civilization,* Princeton University Press, Princeton, New Jersey, 1972.

8. Coomaraswami, A.K., *Hinduism and Buddhism,* Philosophical Library, New York, 1943.

9. Govinda, A.L., *Creative Meditation and Multi-Dimensional Consciousness,* The Theosophical Publishing House, Wheaton, Illinois, 1976.

10. Chuang Tzu, *The Complete Works of Chuang Tzu,* Columbia University Press, New York, 1968.

11. Miyuki, M., *Dying Isagi-Yoku,* Journal of Humanistic Psychology, Vol. 18, No. 4, Fall 1978.

12. Govinda, A.L., *op. cit.,* p. 174.

13. Suzuki, Shunryu, *Zen Mind, Beginners Mind,* Walker/Weatherhill, New York, 1970.

14. Wallace, Robert and Benson, Herbert, "The Physiology of Meditation," *Scientific American,* February 1972 (226: 84-90).

15. Benson, Herbert, et al., "Historical and Clinical Considerations of the Relaxation Response," *American Scientist,* July 1977, 65.

16. Huxley, Aldous, *Island,* Harper and Row, New York, 1962.

17. Govinda, *op. cit.,* p. 221.

18. Blofeld, J., *Taoism—The Road to Immortality,* Shambhala, Boulder, 1978.

19. Watts, Alan, *Cloud Hidden, Whereabouts Unknown,* Pantheon Books, New York, 1973.

20. Easwaran, E., *The Mantram Handbook,* Nilgiri Press, Berkeley, California, 1977.

21. Tarthang Tulku, "Transmuting Energies through Breath," *Crystal Mirror,* Vol. 3 (Annual Journal, Dharma Publishing Co.), Berkeley, 1974.

22. Meyendorff, John, *St. Gregory Palamas and Orthodox Spirituality,* St. Vladimir's Seminary Press, Paris, 1974.

ACKNOWLEDGEMENTS

The meditative practices described in this book originated from and were first given at workshops of the Clear Light Society, Boston, Massachusetts. (Patricia Shelton Harvey, Executive Director).

I am supported in my studies of thanatology and the whole human condition by the Associates in Thanatology, especially Patricia Green, Joe Green, Hulen Kornfeld, Bodo Reichenbach, Claire M. Hinman, Maureen Freedgood, Allen Parker and the Center on Technology and Society.

Acknowledgement is made to the following for permission to reproduce these illustrations:

The Cosmic Web (Fig. 1) reprinted from *TAO*, by Philip Rawson and Laszlo Legeza, Bounty Books, New York, 1978, (Thames & Hudson, Ltd.).

Kuan-Yin (Fig. 2) reprinted from Bookmark *S.Y.D.O.*, P.O. Box 994, Ojai Valley, California.

Yin-Yang (Fig. 3) Reprinted by special arrangement with Shambhala Publications Inc., 1920 13th Street, Boulder, Colorado 80302, from *The Tao of Physics* ©1975 by Fritjof Capra

Dancing Shiva (Fig. 4) Capra, Ibid.

For permission to use quoted passages, acknowledgement is also made to the following:

Harper and Row, Publishers, Inc., for a passage from *Island*, by Aldous Huxley, copyright 1962.

John Weatherhill, Inc., for the chapter "Nirvana the Waterfall," from *Zen Mind, Beginner's Mind*, by Shunryu Suzuki, copyright 1970.

THE AUTHOR

Richard W. Boerstler is a psychotherapist in private practice in Watertown, Massachusetts. His education was at Tufts University where he graduated in 1945 with a Bachelor of Science degree in psychology. In 1946 he did advanced studies in child psychology in Florence, Italy, and worked for many years in the insurance industry as an investigator. In 1978 he founded Associates in Thanatology, a collective of educators and health professionals specializing in transpersonal counseling in grief, loss, pain and death education.

He currently specializes as a practitioner in thanatology offering assistance in the anxieties and fears often associated with life-threatening disease.

He has lectured widely and given workshops at universities, hospitals, hospices and churches.

APPENDIX

During the preparation of this book we were invited to make a presentation at the annual conference of the Forum for Death Education and Counseling in Boston, November 6–8, 1981. The abstract follows:

Abstract: Meditation and the Dying Process

Ancient traditions have employed powerful meditative practices at the time of death. We will explore one of these practices originating in Tibetan medicine, which relied upon specially trained practitioners in the science of consciousness. The concern was to maintain "clear mind and peaceful heart." This was accomplished by the sharing of a cross meditational technique that brought about a very deep state of relaxation.

Studies in autonomic nervous system response and in the physiology of pain now indicate that stress reduction is becoming a necessary modality in modern health care. We describe in this presentation a transpersonal breathing and meditative procedure to deal with anxieties and stress associated with life-threatening illness. We call this procedure "co-meditation." This method is neutral in that it involves no religious or belief system and brings the psychological and physiological effects of the meditative state to patients who have never meditated as well as to meditators. These effects are reported to be a deep muscle relaxation, an alert mental state, lowered metabolic rate, slower heart and respiration rate, lower lactate blood level, increase in skin resistance (G.S.R.) and increase in Alpha Brain Waves.

It is important to understand the relationship between breathing and consciousness. Most meditative disciplines involve the use of breath in a particular manner to effect a stilling of the mind. These disciplines have long been known to be a specific means of letting go of the fears and anxieties that assault the mind.

By creating a certain state of mind the transpersonal approach presented here evokes a certain breathing pattern. Conversely by creating a certain breathing pattern a certain state of mind is evoked.

As practitioners in Thanatology we have become aware that a

fundamental need of the dying patient is not being met. We describe this need as that of transcendence and identity. We have found that this type of meditation meets that need by centering the patient. At the same time this meditation gives the caregiver a necessary task to perform during the dying process, thereby making him/her a part of the holistic life/death transformation.

This technique introduces a shared breathing pattern between care-giver and patient in a specific manner which brings about the mind-body effects noted above. The slower ideation and mentation accompanying this procedure is of great importance in the reduction of anxiety in terminal illness. We encourage further studies and research of this psycho-biological response and welcome all criticism and comment.